Pretty Poetry

ANDREA MITCHUM

Copyright © 2023 Andrea Mitchum

All rights reserved.

No part of this book may be reproduced, stored in a retrieval system, or transmitted, in any form or by any means, electronic, mechanical, photocopying, recording, or otherwise, without prior written permission from the publisher, except for brief quotations embodied in critical reviews and certain other noncommercial uses permitted by copyright law.

ISBN: 978-1-962204-08-8

CONTENTS

🌻

HAIKU	1
DIAMANTÉ	3
LIMERICK POETRY	5
ACROSTIC	7
FREE VERSE	9
SONNETS	12
CINQUAIN	15
EPITAPH	19
ODE	21

Haiku

Haiku is a type of short form poetry originally from Japan. Traditional Japanese haiku usually consist of three phrases composed of 17 phonetic units in a 5, 7, 5 pattern. Haiku poetry include a kireji, or "cutting word"; and a kigo, or seasonal reference.

Phrase 1:   5 syllables
Phrase 2:   7 syllables
Phrase 3:   5 syllables

Winding Waves

Winding waves find me
Searching for unending shells
Treasures of the Sea.

Diamanté

Diamanté is a poem in the shape of a diamond usually about two opposite ideas, for example summer and winter. It is an unrhymed seven line shape poem. There are seven lines with specifics per line. A diamanté will begin with a subject and describe it using adjectives then shift to the opposite idea of the subject by the end of the poem.

Diamante

The first and last lines contain just one word.

The second and sixth lines have two words.

The third and fifth lines have three words.

Lines 1,4, and 7 contain nouns.

Lines 2 and 6 contain adjectives.

Lines 3 and 5 contain verbs.

Graceful Giants

Orcas
Intelligent, Apex
Singing, Playing, Frolicking
Pacific, Atlantic, Indian, Arctic
Rolling, Diving, Consuming
Curious, Intimidating
Shark

Limerick Poetry

A limerick is a five-line poem that consists of a single stanza, an AABBA rhyme scheme, and whose subject is a short story of sorts.

Lines 1, 2, and 5 contain the same number of syllables, usually between eight to ten syllables, and rhyme.

Lines 3 and 4 are shorter with only five or six syllables, and rhyme.

Subject matter can be people, animals, and places, anything from your imagination.

Goat's Raincoat

Once in your life you might meet a goat

With fuzzy fur and a red motor boat

He might convince you to a race

Or maybe try to fly to space

Whatever happens make sure to wear your favorite coat!

Acrostic

An acrostic poem utilizes the first letter in a word to create words that describe the topic. The topic can be anything, nouns, verbs, or adjectives.

Write the word vertically and think of words that describe the first line or topic.

Andrea

A- Angelic

N- Nieve

D- Driven

R- Responsible

E- Energetic

A- Absolutely Funny

Honolulu

Honolulu
Awesome sunsets
White waves
Awesome beaches
Invigorating
In the Pacific

Free Verse

Free verse poems have no regular meter or rhythm and do not follow a proper rhyme scheme. Free verse poems do not have any set rules.

This type of poem is based on normal pauses and natural rhythmical phrases, as compared to the rules of normal poetry with rhymes and rhythms.

Check out Walt Whitman and T. S. Eliot.

Magical Spheres

I never thought I'd see a magical sphere
Flying ever so quietly above the horizon
Where is your captain?
Where is your ship?
Please, don't take me unless you are friendly
Space is the final frontier or is it?
Maybe the ocean is the final frontier
Where lights can be seen but sounds go silent
When silvery metal objects dive in our seas
Are you our friends? Did you come back to help us?
In my mind, I exponentially hope so............

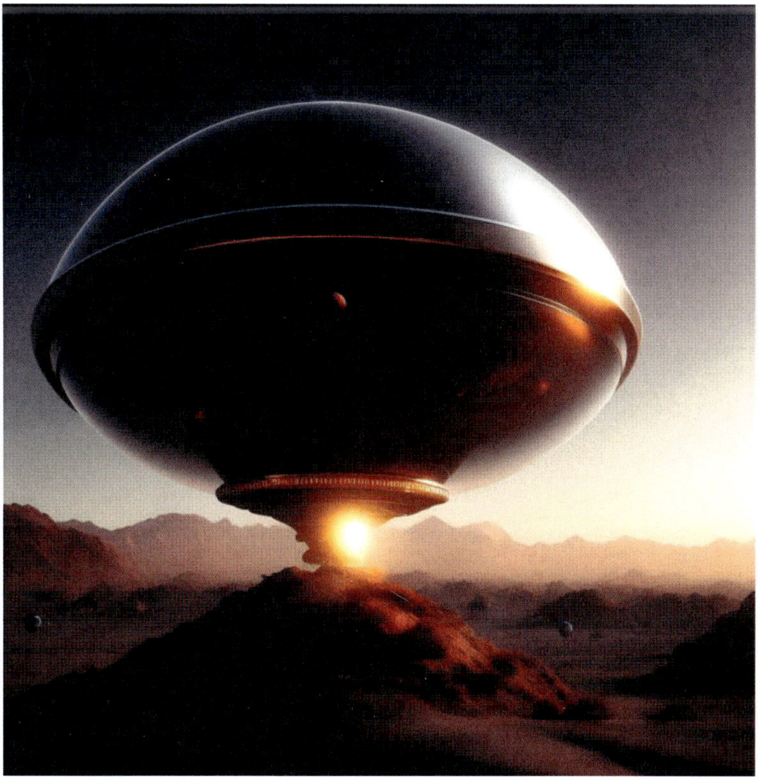

Sonnets

The sonnet is a fourteen-line poem written in iambic pentameter, using one of several rhyme schemes, and adhering to a tightly structured thematic organization. The name is taken from the Italian sonetto, which means "a little sound or song."

<u>Characteristics of a Sonnet:</u>
14 lines long
Variable rhyme scheme
Strict metrical construction

One should understand the building block of all sonnet poetry: iambic pentameter, a metric line very common in traditional poetry.

An Iamb is a beat in poetry made up of an unstressed syllable followed by a stressed syllable – for example, re-WRITE or re-FRAIN. Pentameter means that there are five metrical feet per line or ten total syllables.

The Shakespearean sonnet is typically broken into three quatrains and one couplet. The resulting Shakespearean sonnet rhyme scheme is: abab, cdcd, efef, gg.

To review

Themes: Sonnet topics generally express a strong emotion, such as love.

Rhyme scheme – The rhyming pattern is abab, cdcd, efef, gg.

Structure – Sonnets are fourteen lines long, with a rhyme scheme of abab, cdcd, efef, gg, and with an iambic pentameter.

Iambic pentameter – Most of Shakespeare's sonnets use iambic pentameter, which means there are ten syllables per line.

Friendship with Seri

Shall I compare thee to a summer's day?
Thou art 'round 98 degrees as well
I seek to help thee order a latte,
And waketh thee, thy constant alarm 'bell.

Sometimes too soft thy Air Pods play thy iTunes
So turn it up do I at thy command
When Bruno Mars thy Uptown Funk doth croon,
And thy volume button eludes thy hand.

Lo, thy loyal assistant shall not fade,
My memory shall never fail to thee remind
For to assist thee is my only trade,
In Maps, the best of routes for thee I find.

So long as thy words doth seek to reach me
So long I stay, your assistant, Seri.

Cinquain

A cinquain is a five line poem. So, each stanza would contain five lines usually written in iambic meter- an unstressed syllable followed by a stressed syllable.

In an iambic pentameter there are usually ten syllables. A word is iambic if the first syllable is short and unstressed whereas the second syllable is long and stressed.

An example would be Shakespeare's, Romeo and Juliet. Read it aloud and listen for unstressed and stressed syllabications.

Blank verse is the name for poetry that is written in iambic pentameter but no rhyme scheme is utilized.

The following are guidelines for writing a cinquain:

1. Line 1: One word about your topic for your poem, use two syllables.
2. Line 2: Think of two adjectives that describe your topic, use four syllables.
3. Line 3: Write three action verbs that describe your topic, use six syllables.

4. Line 4: Write four words that describe a feeling about your topic, use eight syllables.
5. Line 5: Use a word that is a specific synonym for your topic in line one, use only two syllables.

My Muse- Music

Music
Vinyl, Records
Freeing, Calming, Playing
Sounds of freedom in the night air
Skynyrd

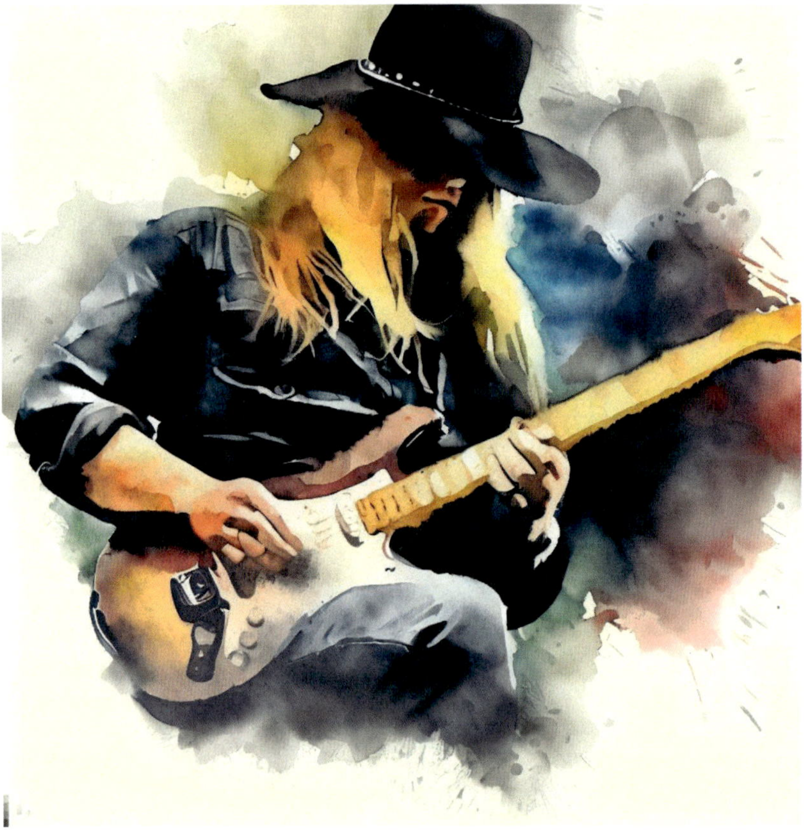

Epitaph

The term epitaph refers to a statement, usually a short one, about a person that is deceased.

An epitaph is sometimes poetic but usually is just a short statement about the deceased person. The word. "Epitaph" comes from Greek etymology, "Epitaphios" which means funeral oration. An epitaph is meant to honor a person. Disney's Haunted House has funny examples of epitaphs on the tombstones before entering the Haunted House.

A person's epitaph is written on their tombstone!

Examples:

Grandmother

A woman of virtue and endless affection.

Mother

Rest in peace may your heart be healed.

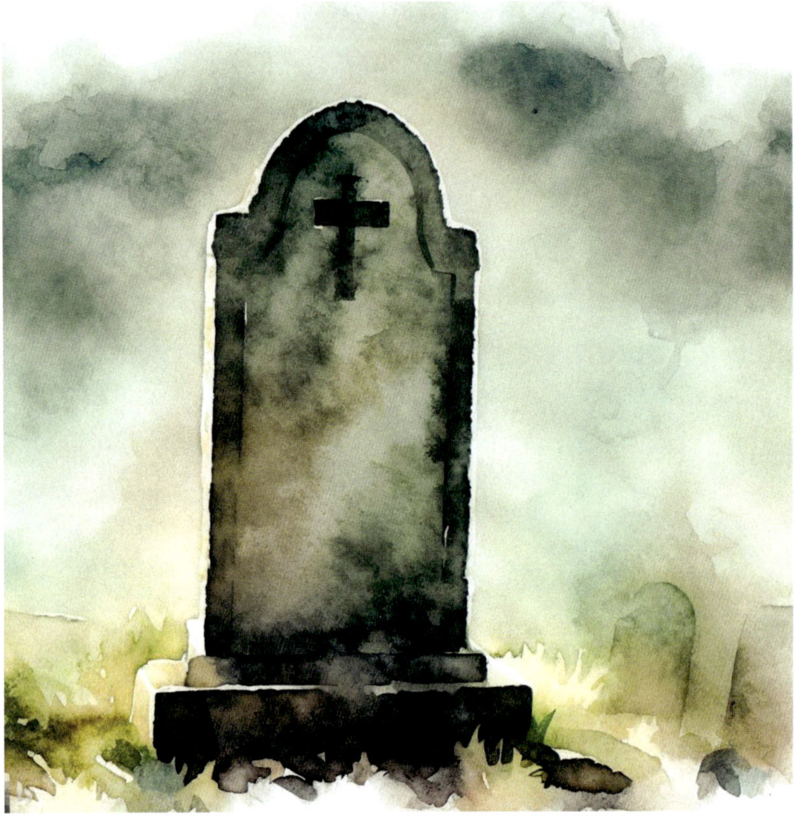

Ode

An ode is written to express higher thoughts about a subject that one holds in high regard.

An ode may rhyme or be unrhymed. Historically there are three types of odes: Pindaric odes, Horatian odes, and Irregular odes which follow no standard pattern of rhyme scheme.

A Pindaric ode is written using three stanzas of which two contain the same structure. Read poetry by the Greek poet Pindar to get a feel for this type of ode.

A Horatian ode follows the same rhyme scheme and meter. Horace, the Roman poet, utilized this type of ode.

Rhyming is not necessary for an ode but many traditional odes do utilize a rhyme scheme.

Many of them also begin with, "Ode to……".

Ode to Rock n Roll

Lynyrd Skynyrd's music has danced through five decades of moving time

Ronnie, Cassie, Steve, Allen, and Gary now in Heaven lifting their voices to God

Is there a more loving band to be in than the Sounds of Worship?

We know we will see them again, it is just a matter of time.

I love the music of Lynyrd Skynyrd- recorded sounds drift throughout my house to remind me that the sounds I hear will live on. Long live Rock n Roll. Long live Skynyrd Nation!!!

In this book of Pretty Poetry, my desire was to share different types of simple poetry.

Poetry is a creative outlet for personal expression. You may follow the rules or you may break the rules. Being creative to me is more about expressing your emotions, thoughts, hurts, accomplishments, or life in general rather than following specific rules. If you like to use specific formats then have fun!

Write daily if you like to write poetry and/or just to express yourself, or if you enjoy reading poetry, then I do hope you enjoy my book of pretty poetry!

This book is dedicated to the members of my favorite band, Lynyrd Skynyrd, that are now in Heaven. I never got to meet them but I enjoy the southern sounds that they have shared with the world for 50 years. Music does make the world a much happier place!

Made in United States
Orlando, FL
10 August 2023